ИСТОРИЯ ЧИСЕЛ

THE NUMBER STORY

SMALL BOOK ONE

ENGLISH - RUSSIAN

Numbers Teach Children
Their Number Names

written and illustrated by

MISS ANNA

Early Reader Edition of *The Number Story 1*
Bronze Medal Winner, 2016 Wishing Shelf Book Award

Library of Congress Control Number: 2018902040

Names: Miss Anna, author.
Title: Number story : numbers teach children their number names / Miss Anna.
Description: Portland, OR: Lumpy Publishing, 2018.
Identifiers: ISBN 978-1-945977-16-9| LCCN 2018902040
Summary: The pictures and rhymes present stories which introduce numbers 0-10.
Subjects: LCSH Numeration—English--Russian--Pictorial works--Juvenile literature. | BISAC JUVENILE NONFICTION /
Languages: English--Russian
Classification: LCC QA141.3 .M57 2018 | DDC 513—dc23

Publisher: Lumpy Publishing
Website: www.missannabooks.com
Email: missanna@missannabooks.com

Paperback: ISBN 978-1-945977-16-9
Printed in the U.S.A.   1 3 5 7 9 10 8 6 4 2

Хочешь выучить
числа?

It is very easy and a lot of fun!

Это очень просто и весело!

Say-along our little jingle

Спой вместе с нами песенку

starting from Number One!

И начнем с цифры один!

1

ONE looks like my one finger.

ОДИН

Один выглядит как
мой пальчик.

ONE!
Один!

2

TWO   trails a tail.

ДВА

А у Двух есть хвост.

A TAIL!
ХВОСТ!

3

THREE has bumps.

ТРИ

Три - как верблюд.

Посмотрите на горбы!

4

FOUR carries a sail.

ЧЕТЫРЕ

А четыре это парус!

A SAIL!
Парус!

5

FIVE   is a racing track.

ПЯТЬ

Пять это гоночный трек.

VRooM
Tppp!
1

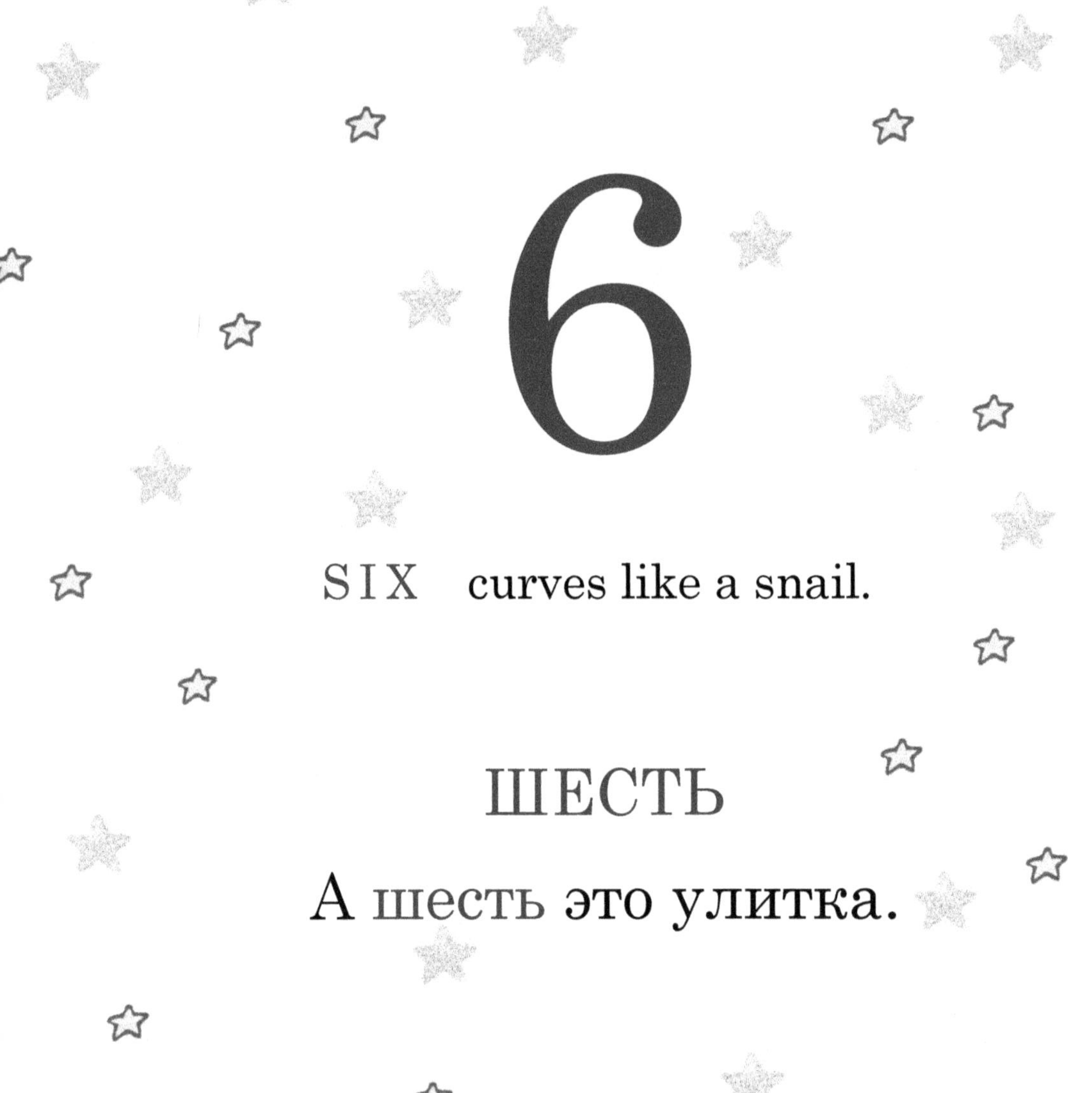

6

SIX curves like a snail.

ШЕСТЬ

А шесть это улитка.

A SNAIL!

Улитка!

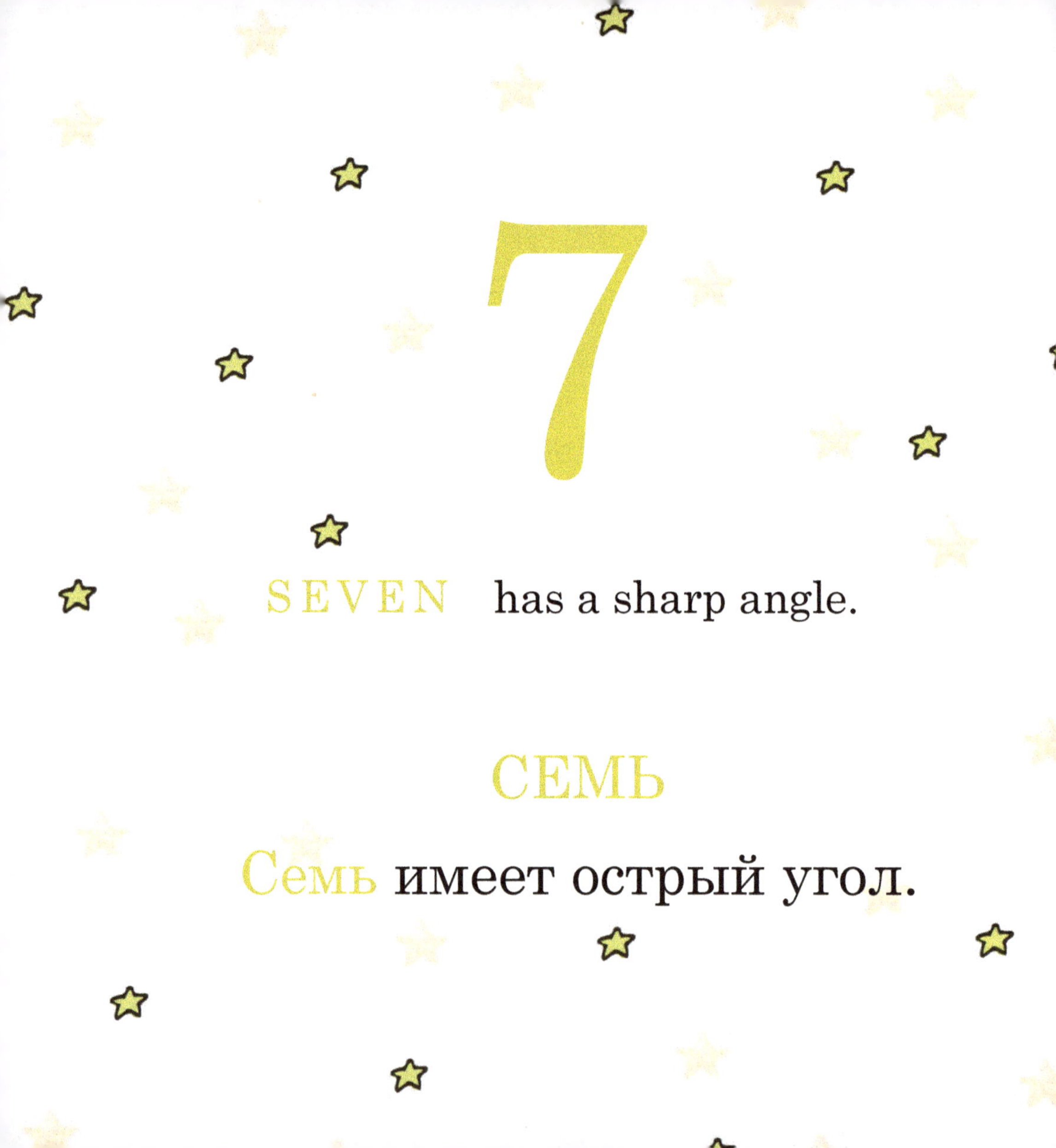

7

SEVEN has a sharp angle.

СЕМЬ

Семь имеет острый угол.

OUCH!
Ауч!

8

E I G H T   is rollercoaster rails.

ВОСЕМЬ

А восемь — американские горки.

Yay!
YIPPEE!

NINE   is a bubble on a stick.

ДЕВЯТЬ

Девять это пузырь на палочке.

A BUBBLE! Пузырь!

10

TEN   is an eye of a whale.

ДЕСЯТЬ

Десять это глаз кита.

WINK!
Подмигивает!

And
И

0

ZERO   is an empty pail.

НУЛЬ

А ноль это пустое ведро.

IT'S
EMPTY!
Пустой!

Thank you for playing with us today.

We had a lot of fun too!

Спасибо, что играл с нами.

Это было очень весело!

We are your Number friends,
Zero to Ten,
Who will be here for you~

Мы твои друзья –
от нуля до десяти.
Мы всегда здесь для тебя!

Bye-bye now!
See you again soon.

А пока до свидания!
До скорой встречи!

The Numbers are *SINGING* too!

To sing-a-long, look for Miss Anna Number Story
at your favorite music store like iTUNES.

MP3

Numbers 0-10
IDENTIFYING
& COUNTING

Numbers 11-20
& Ordinals

first, second, third...

Numbers 0-100
& Place Values

ones, tens, hundreds...

About Clocks
& Telling Time

hours, minutes, seconds

Number Story 1 & 2

isbn: 978-0-996216-48-7

Number Story 3 & 4

isbn: 978-1-945977-01-5

Number Story 5 & 6

isbn: 978-1-945977-06-0

Number Story 7 & 8

isbn: 978-1-949320-40-4

For more Miss Anna books to love,
visit us at

w w w . m i s s a n n a b o o k s . c o m

Numbers are working hard all over the world!
Come Travel the World with Us!

9 781945 977169